This Journal Belongs To:

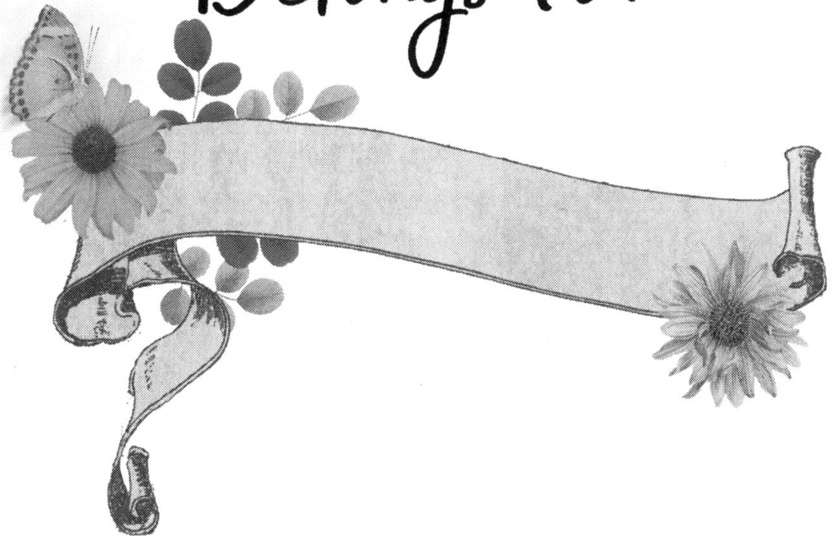

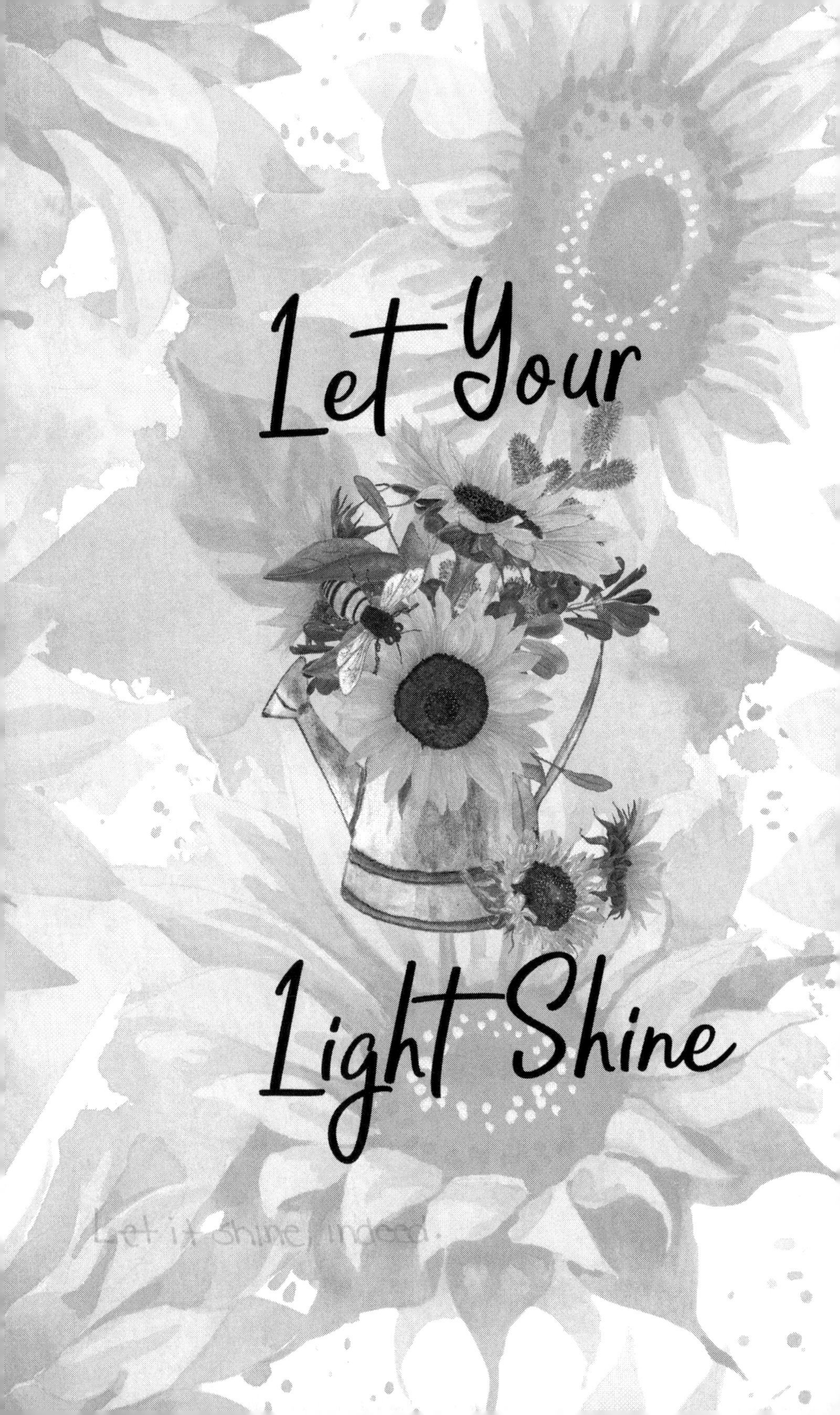
Let Your
Light Shine
Let it shine, indeed.

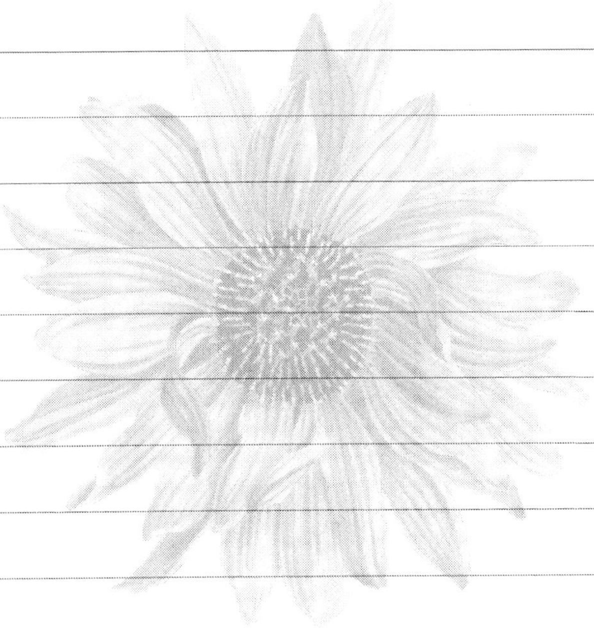

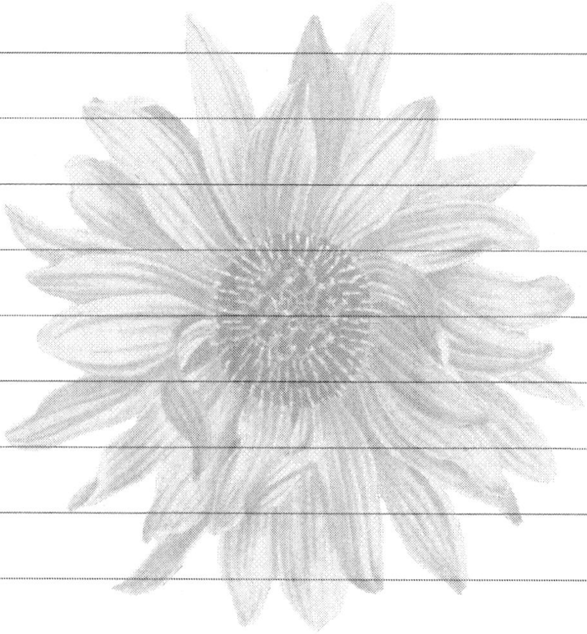

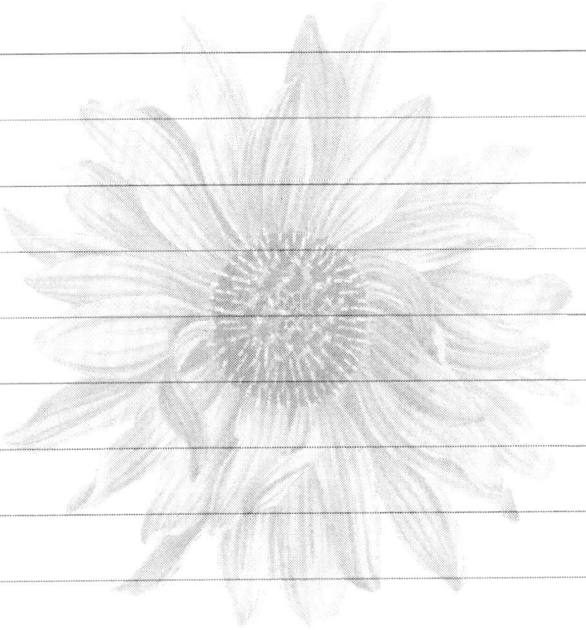

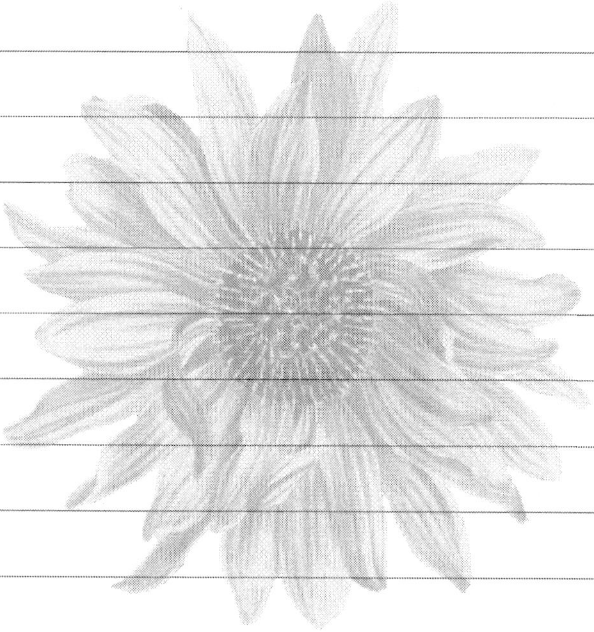

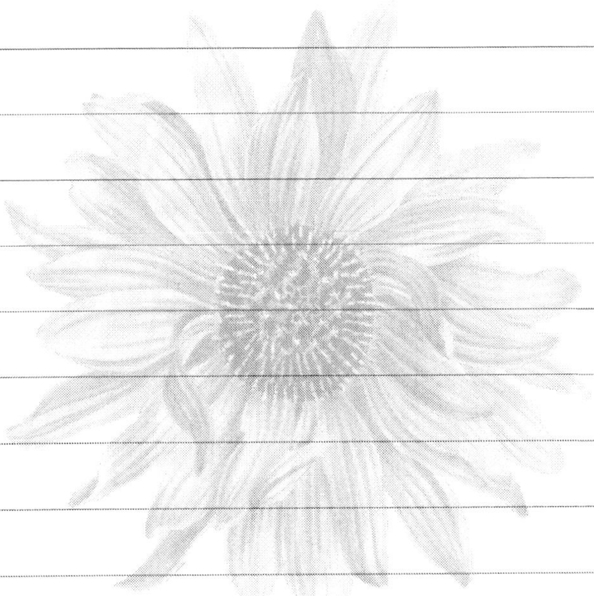

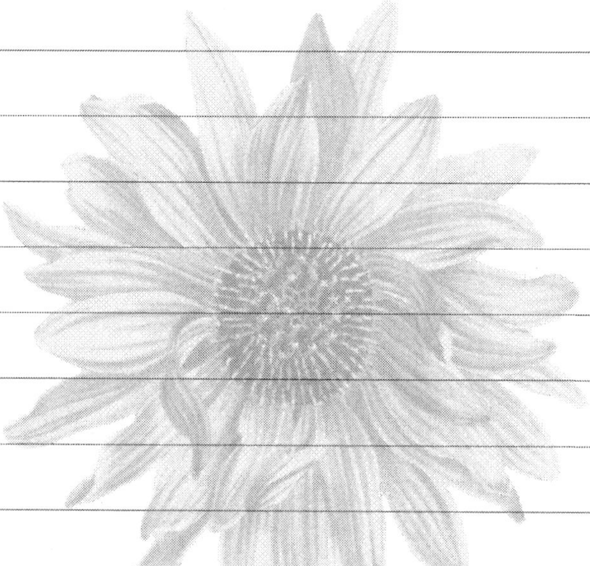

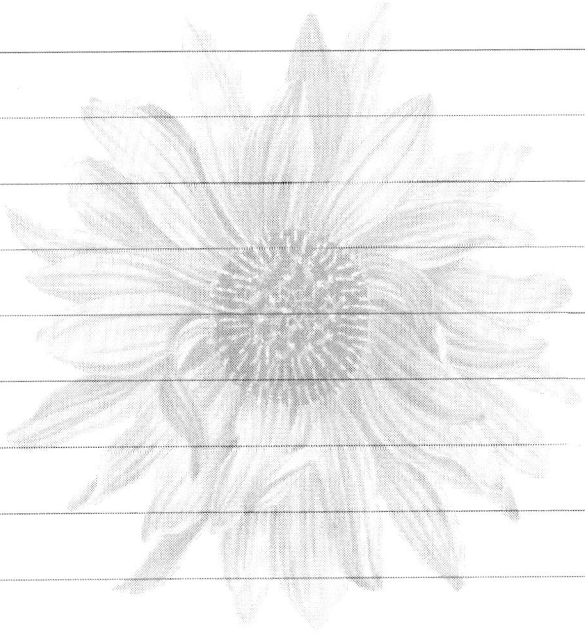

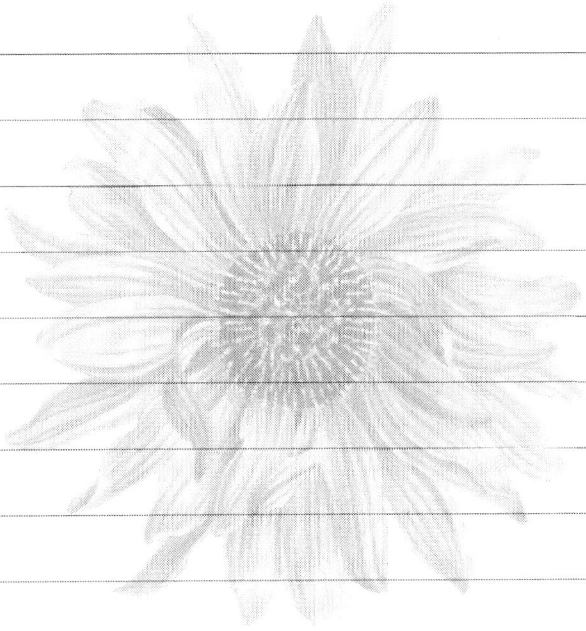

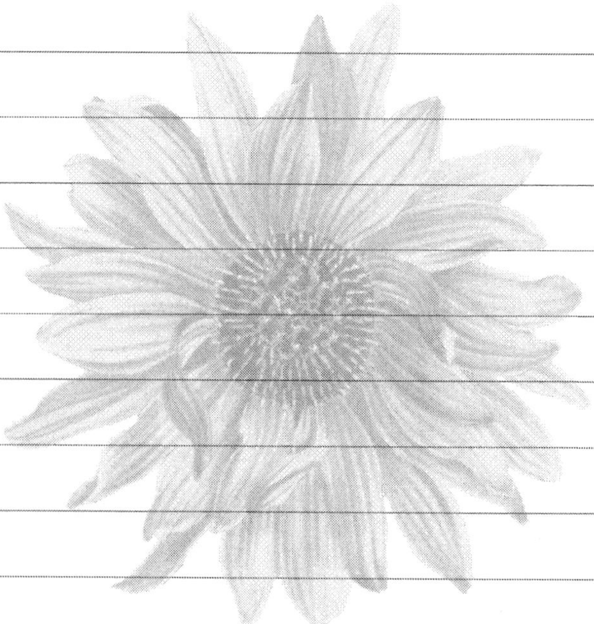

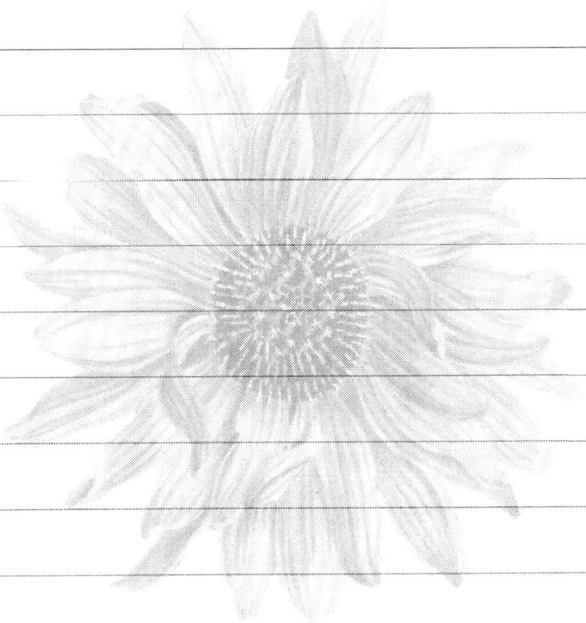

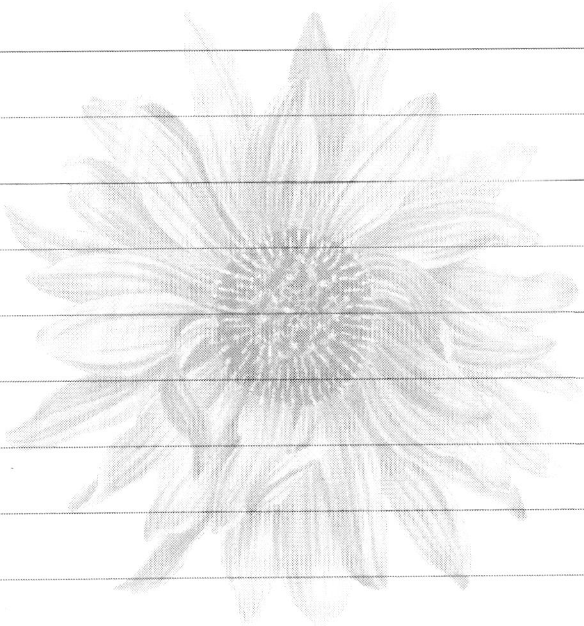

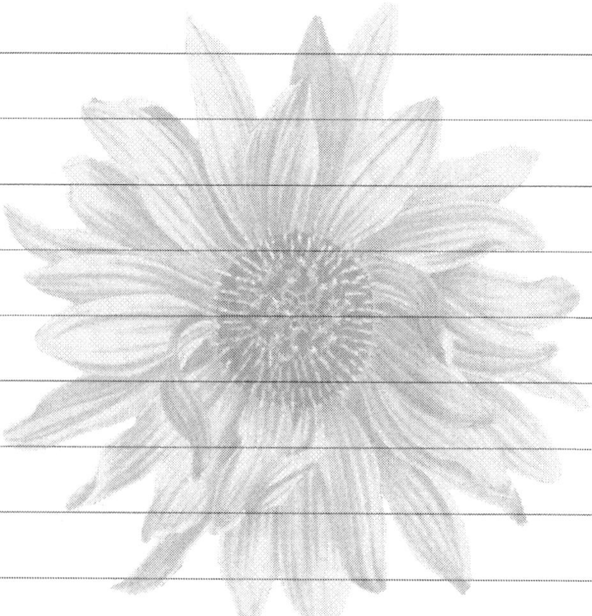

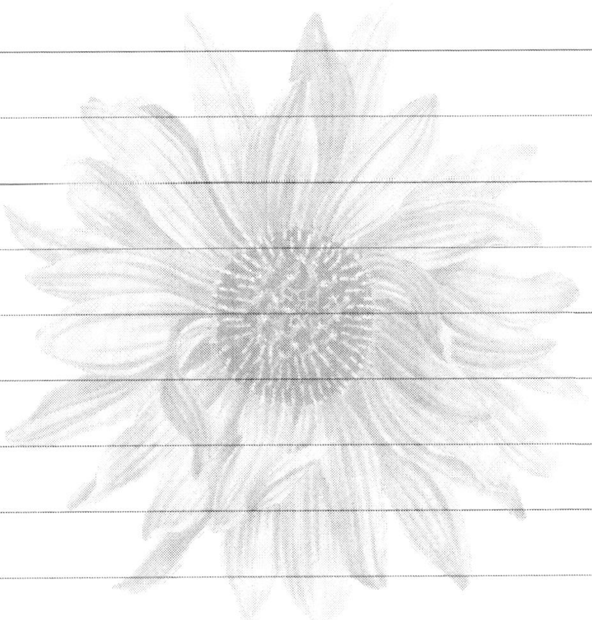

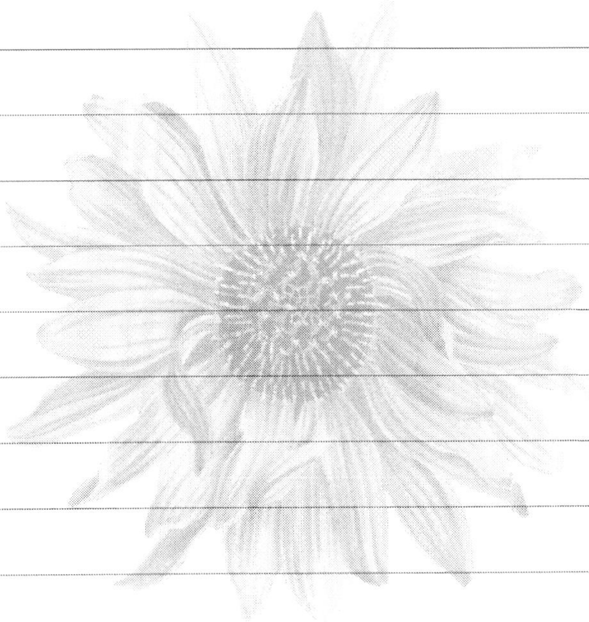

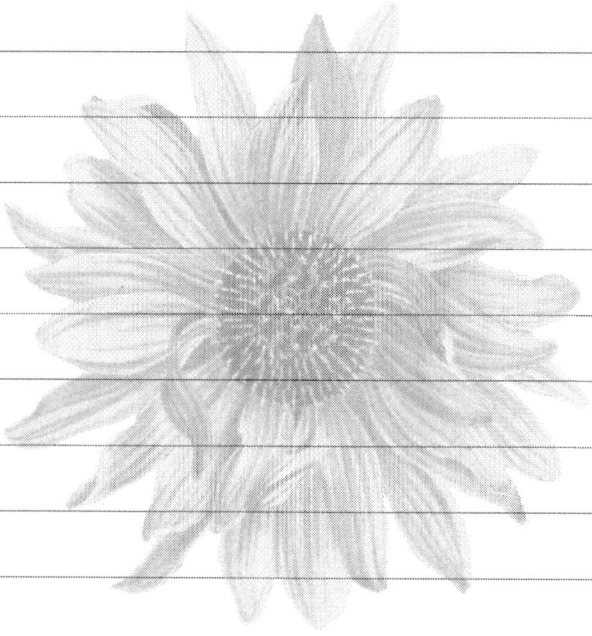

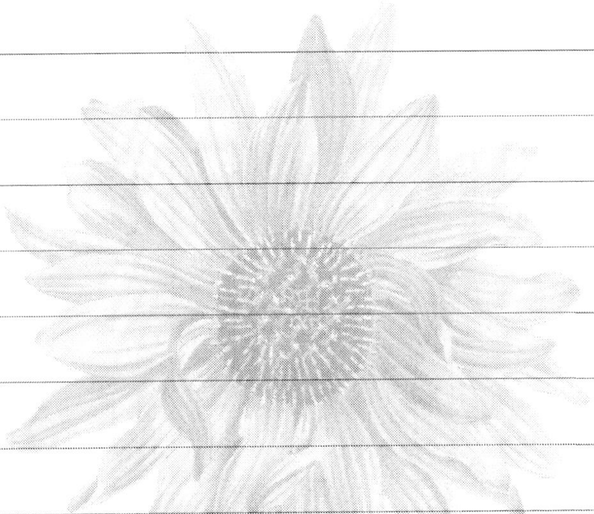

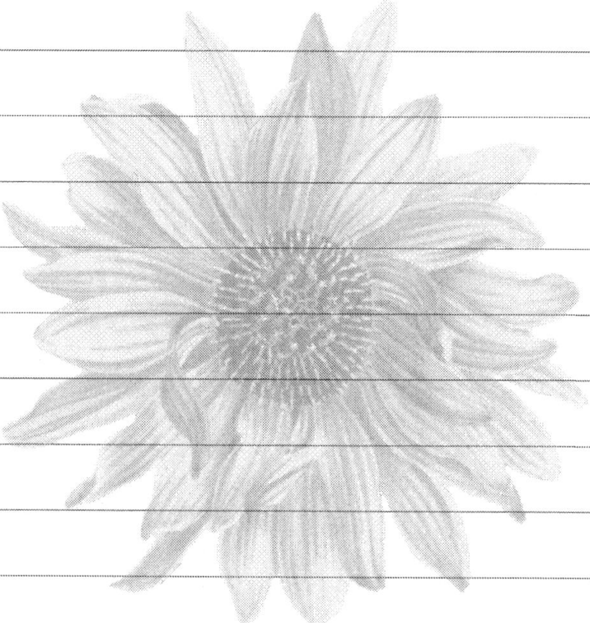

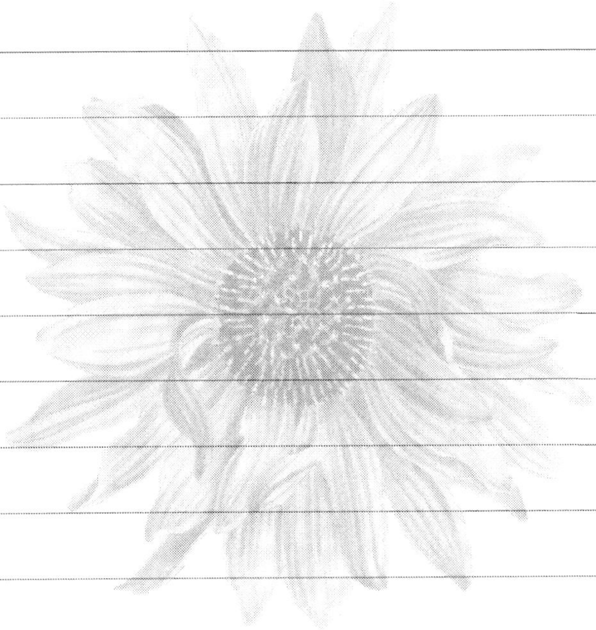

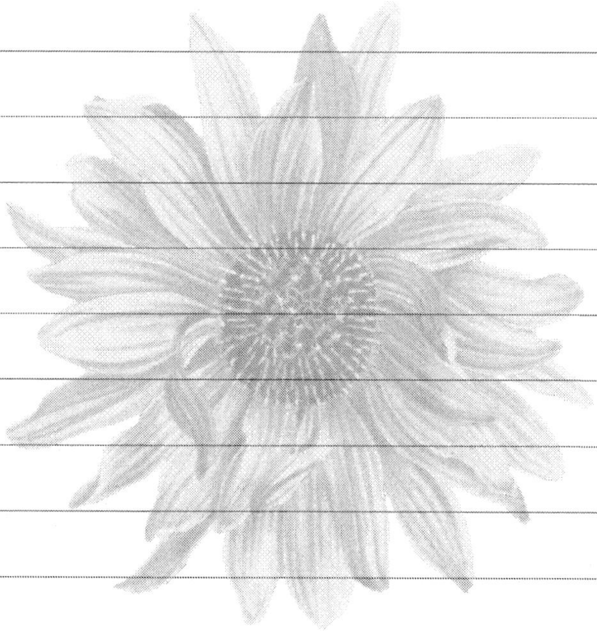

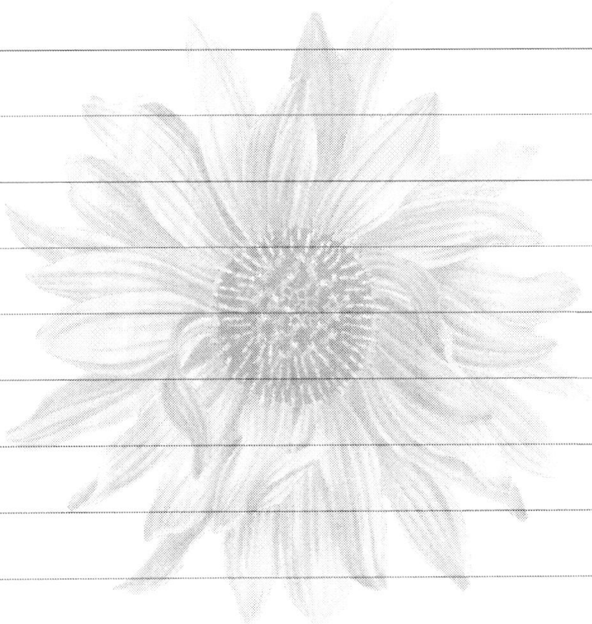

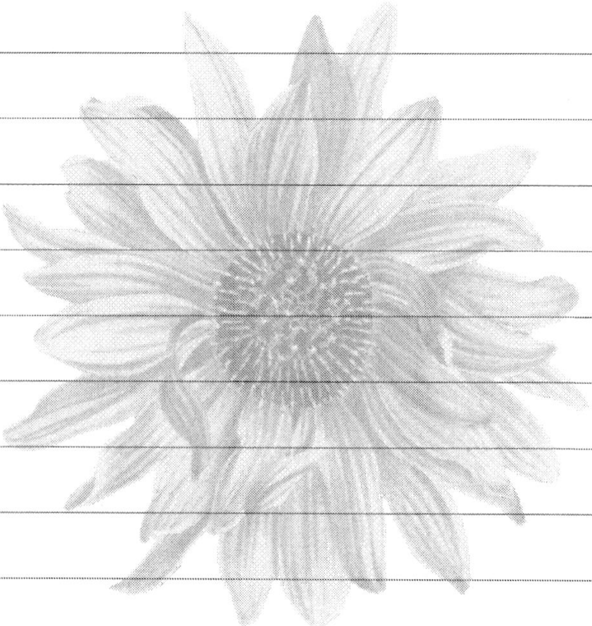

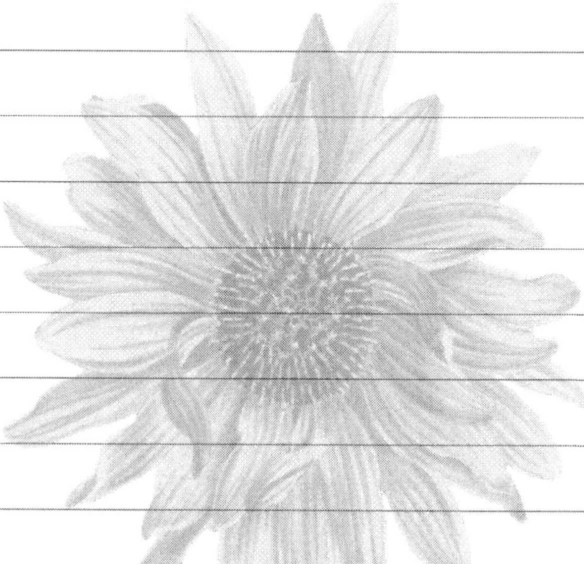

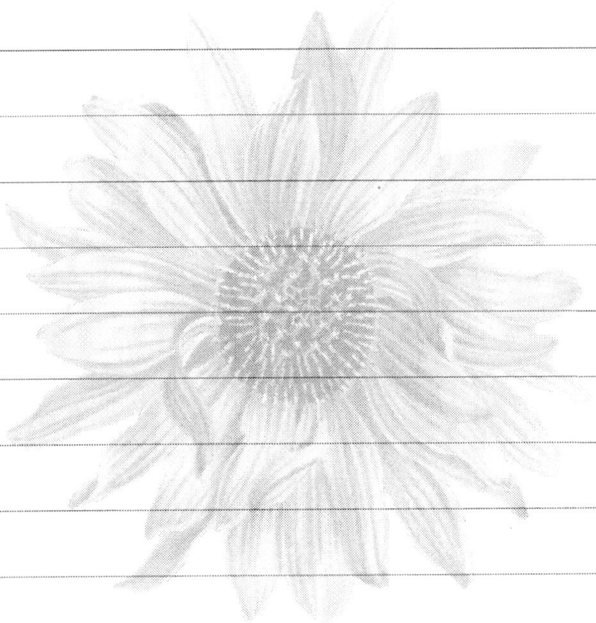

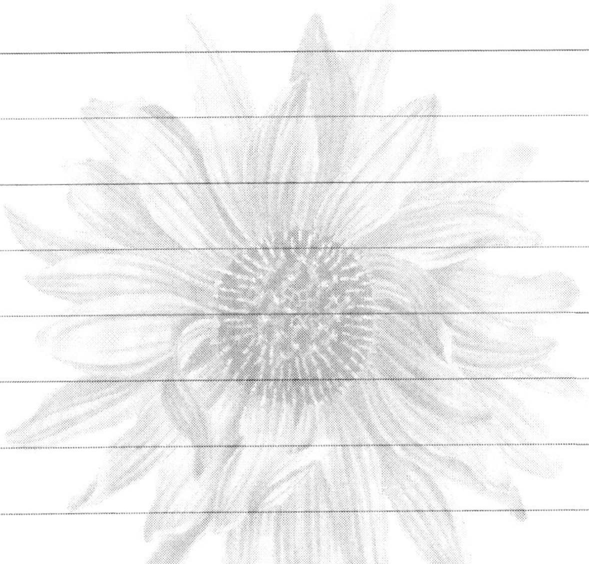

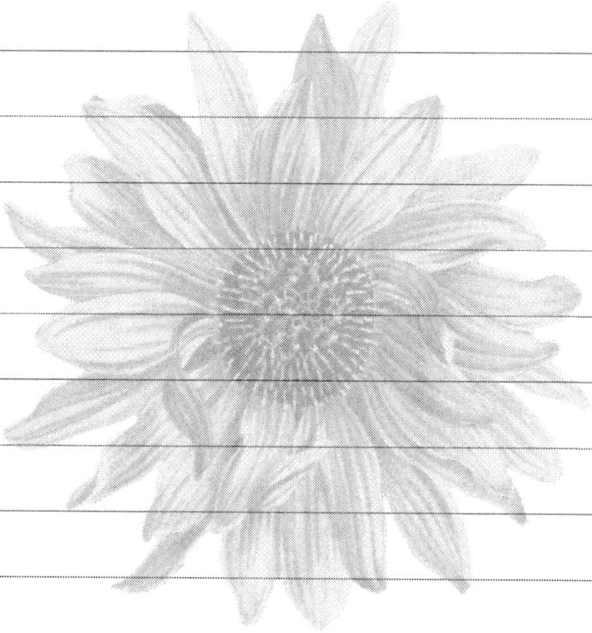

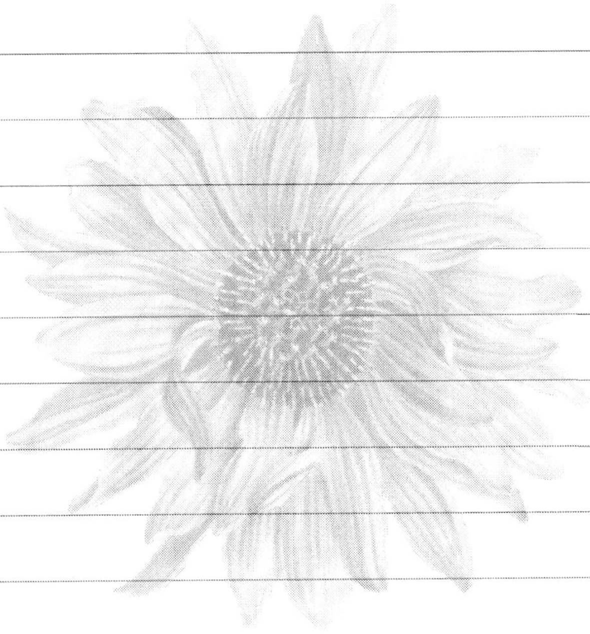

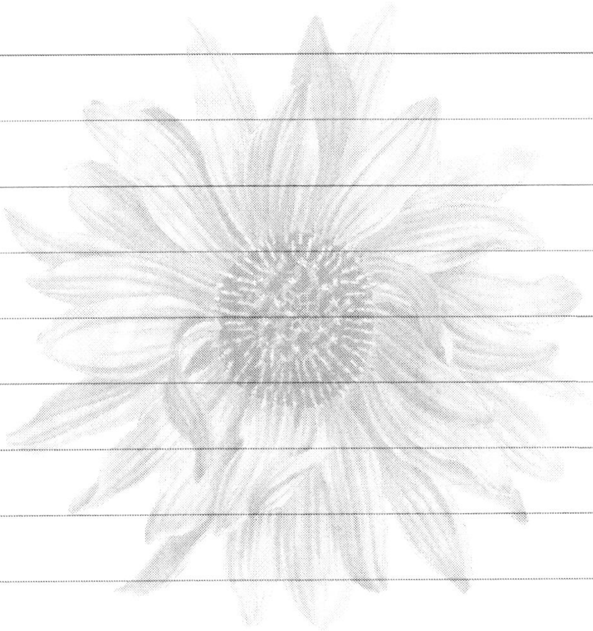

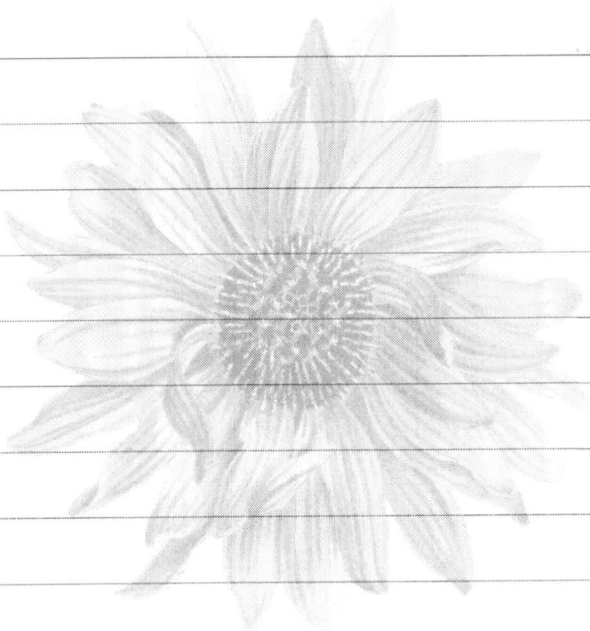

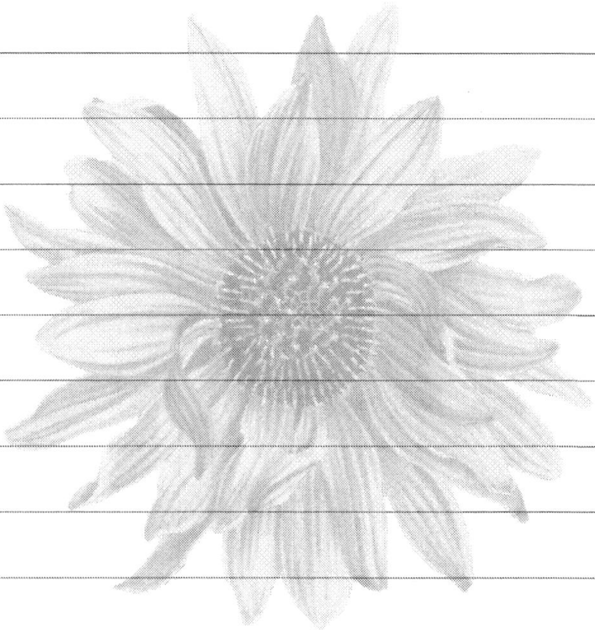

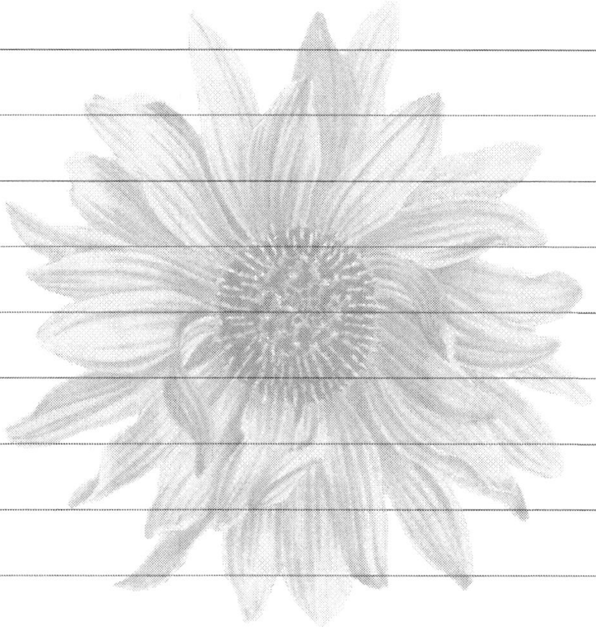

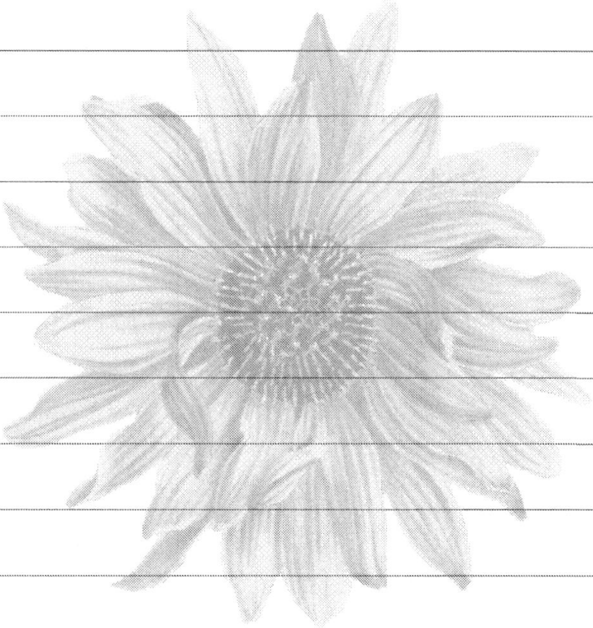

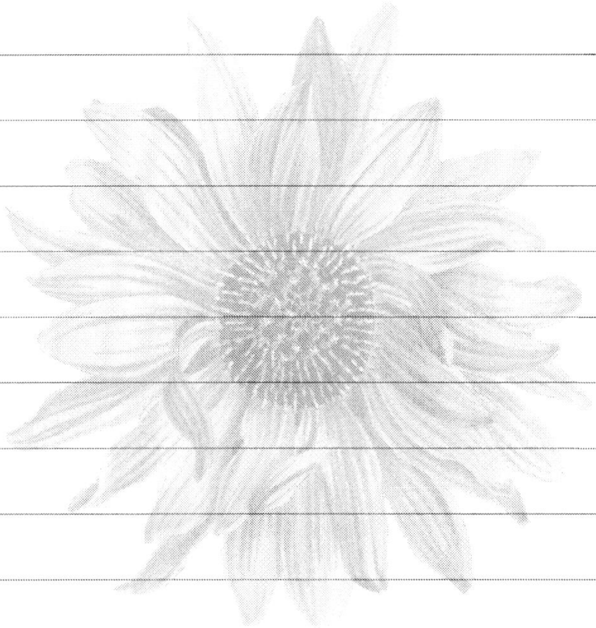

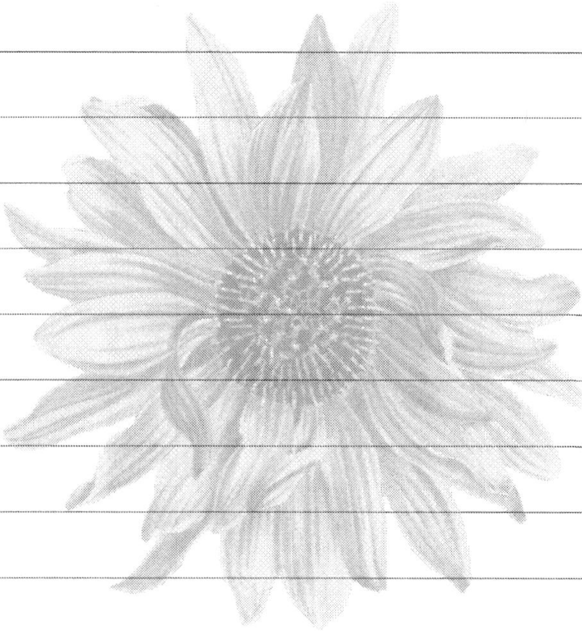

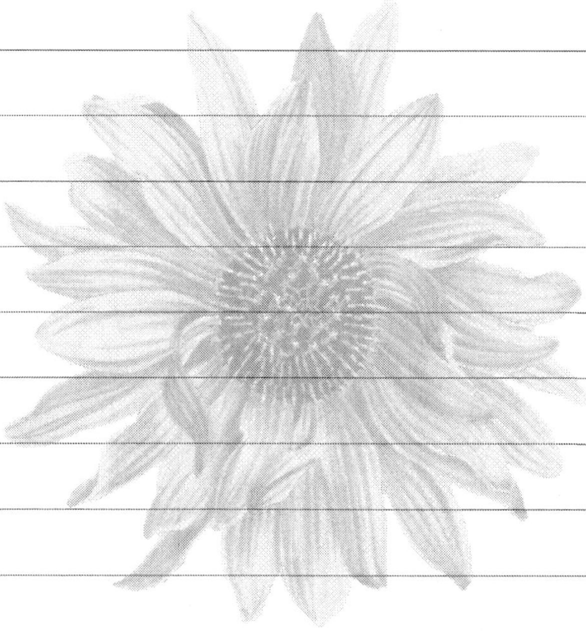

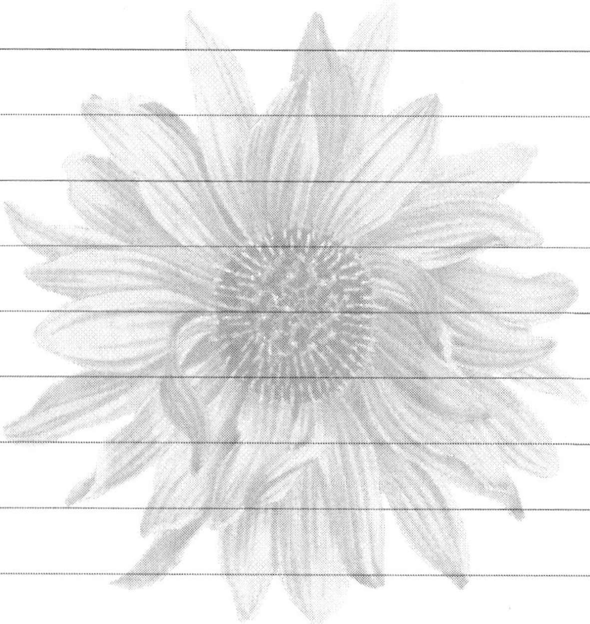

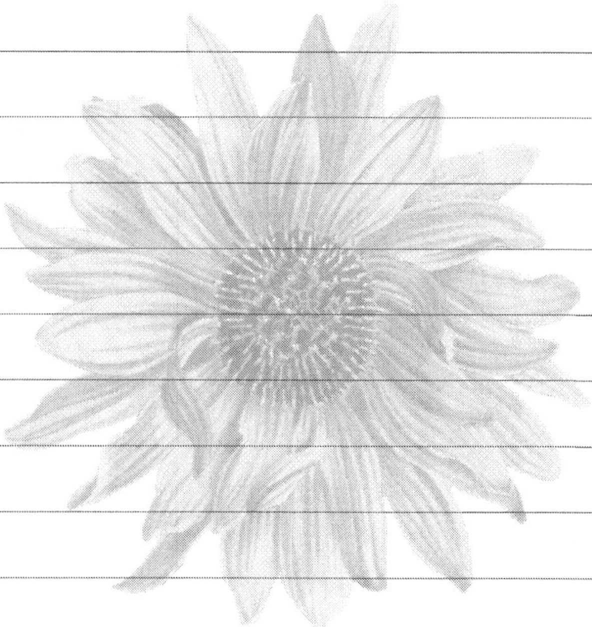

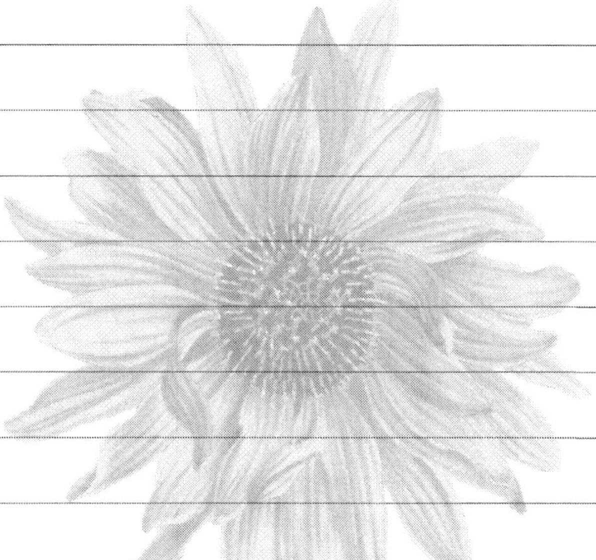

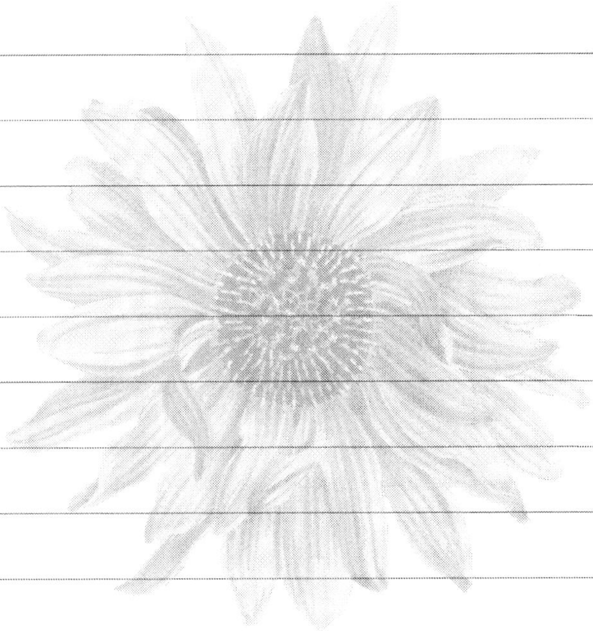

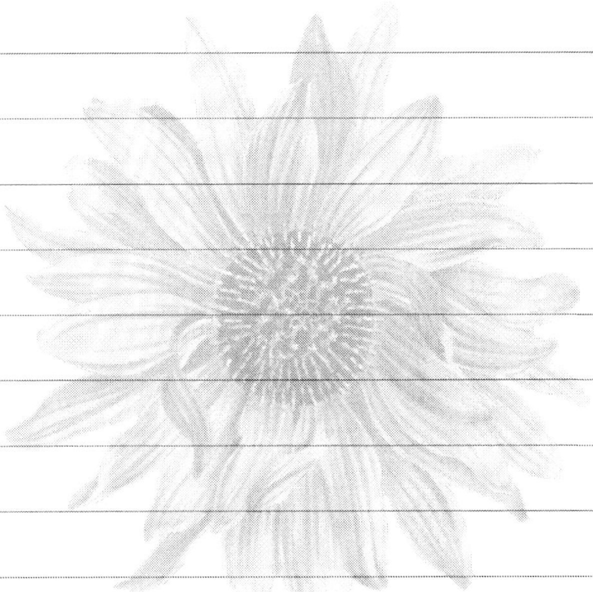

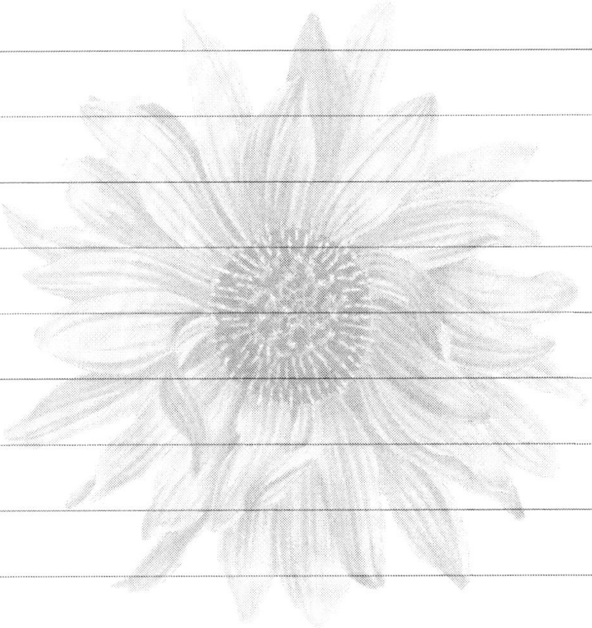

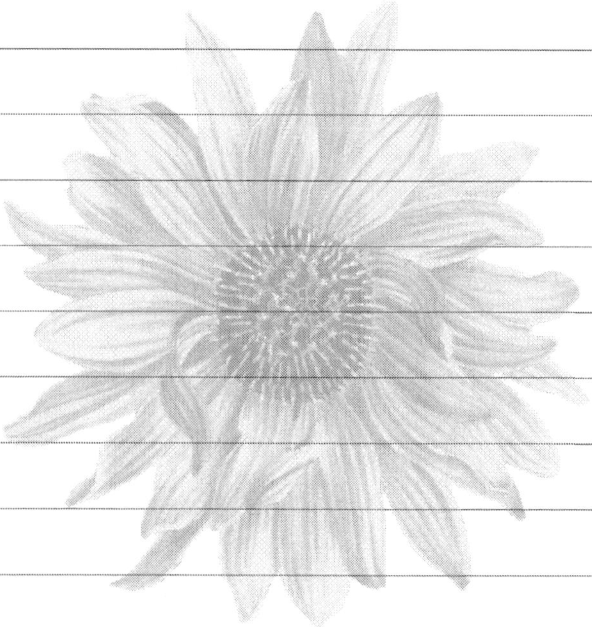

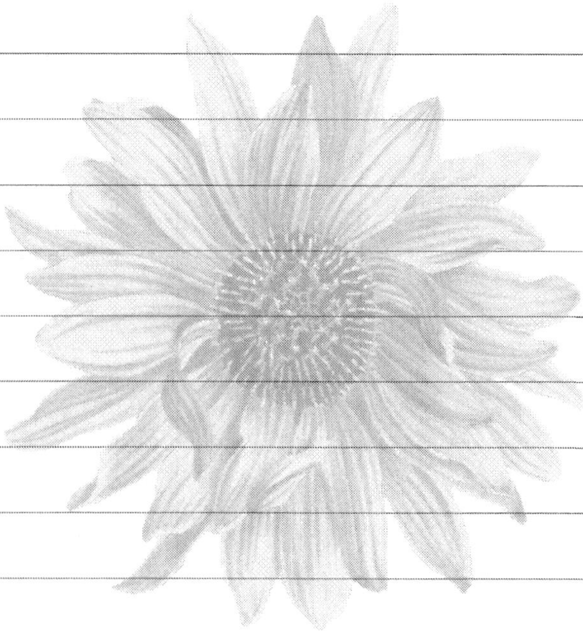

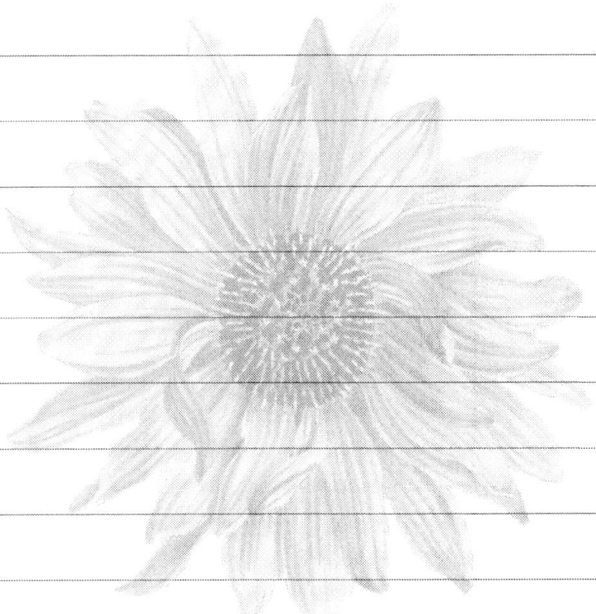

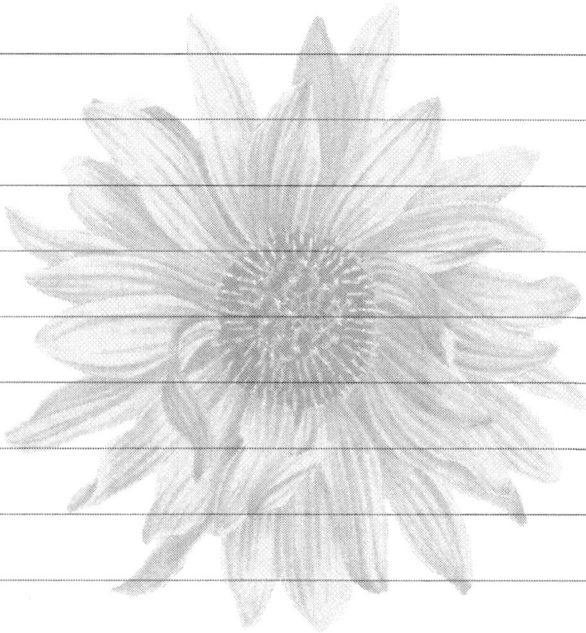

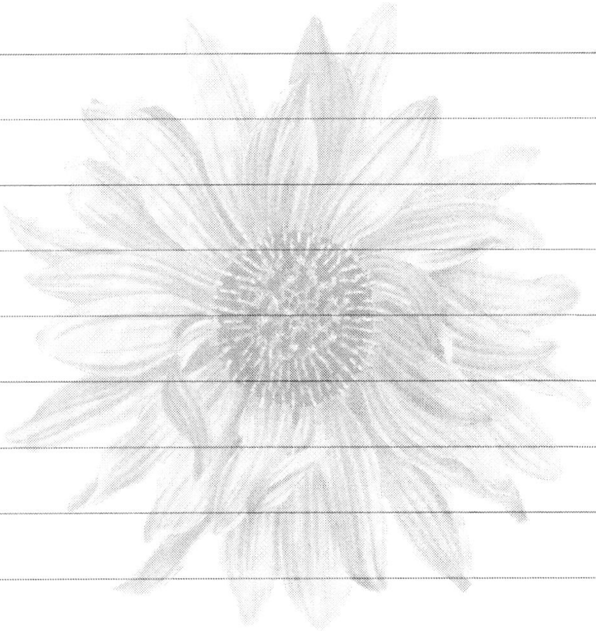

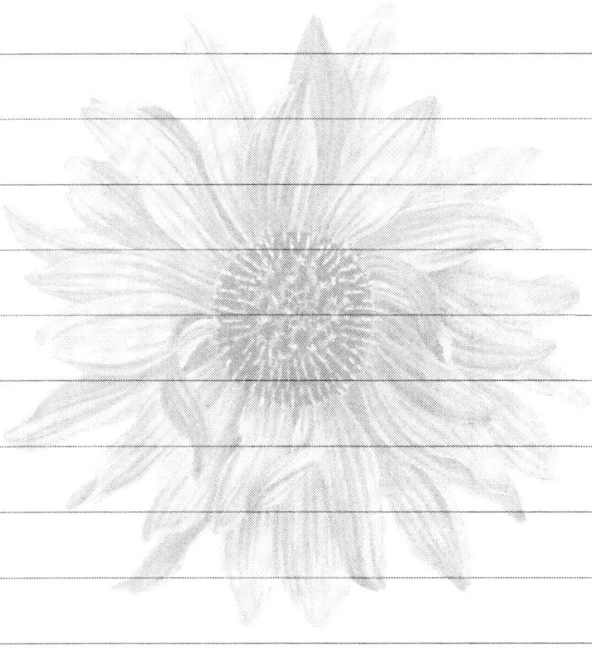

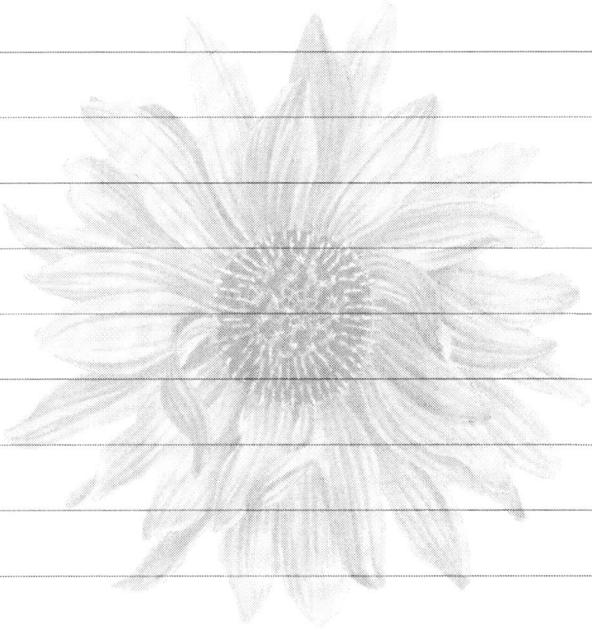

Sunflowers Make Your

Happy

Comment below: do sunflowers make your happy?

Manufactured by Amazon.ca
Bolton, ON

18475126R00068